ST. LOUIS
RAMS

by George Castle

Published by ABDO Publishing Company, 8000 West 78th Street, Edina, Minnesota 55439. Copyright © 2011 by Abdo Consulting Group, Inc. International copyrights reserved in all countries. No part of this book may be reproduced in any form without written permission from the publisher. SportsZone™ is a trademark and logo of ABDO Publishing Company.

Printed in the United States of America,
North Mankato, Minnesota
062010
092010

 THIS BOOK CONTAINS AT LEAST 10% RECYCLED MATERIALS.

Editor: Chrös McDougall
Copy Editor: Nicholas Cafarelli
Interior Design and Production: Christa Schneider
Cover Design: Craig Hinton

Photo Credits: Paul Jasienski/AP Images, cover; NFL Photos/AP Images, title page, 4, 7, 9, 18, 23, 25, 26, 29, 30, 34, 37, 42 (middle and bottom), 43 (middle and bottom); John Gaps III/AP Images, 11; AP Images, 12, 15, 17, 20, 33, 42 (top); James A. Finley/AP Images, 39, 47; Tom Gannam/AP Images, 41, 43 (bottom), 44

Library of Congress Cataloging-in-Publication Data
Castle, George.
  St. Louis Rams / George Castle.
    p. cm. — (Inside the NFL)
  Saint Louis Rams
  ISBN 978-1-61714-029-7
  1. St. Louis Rams (Football team)—History—Juvenile literature. I. Title. II. Title: Saint Louis Rams.
  GV956.S85C37 2011
  796.332'640977866—dc22
                                 2010017459

TABLE OF CONTENTS

CHAPTER 1

THE GREATEST SHOW ON TURF

When the 1999 season rolled around, the St. Louis Rams were in need of some good news. They had been a mostly losing team during the early 1990s while playing in Los Angeles, California. Those losing ways continued when they moved to St. Louis before the 1995 season. Things finally began looking up as the 1999 season approached, however.

The team had brought in veteran coach Dick Vermeil in 1997. The Rams still struggled to a 4–12 record in 1998. But before the 1999 season, the Rams had traded for superstar running back Marshall Faulk. He had four 1,000-yard rushing seasons with the Indianapolis Colts, but a contract dispute forced the team to trade him. All the Rams had to give up were second- and fifth-round picks in the 2000 National Football League (NFL) Draft.

Faulk joined an offense that already had its share of talent. The Rams had also signed

RAMS RUNNING BACK MARSHALL FAULK LOOKS FOR SPACE TO RUN IN SUPER BOWL XXXIV. HE HAD 107 YARDS OF OFFENSE IN THE GAME.

RECORD BREAKER

Marshall Faulk quickly fit in with the Rams. In 1999, he totaled a then-NFL record 2,429 yards of total offense while also scoring 12 touchdowns. That broke Detroit Lions legend Barry Sanders' record of 2,358 all-purpose yards set in 1997. Faulk had 1,381 yards rushing (5.5 yards-per-carry average) and 1,048 yards receiving.

Faulk is the only player to have at least 12,000 rushing yards and 6,000 receiving yards in a career. Among his other unmatched feats are seven two-point conversions, five games of 250-plus yards from scrimmage, and 14 games of 200-plus yards from scrimmage. He is also the only player to record at least 70 rushing touchdowns and 30 or more receiving touchdowns. "He can go from a standing start to full speed faster than anybody I've ever seen," former Colts coach Ted Marchibroda said. Faulk retired in 2007 after missing the 2006 season with injuries.

hometown quarterback Trent Green during that offseason. He had passed for 23 touchdowns the season before with the Washington Redskins. They then selected talented wide receiver Torry Holt with the sixth overall pick in the NFL Draft. He would be paired alongside Pro Bowl wide receiver Isaac Bruce. The pieces were in place for the Rams to have a breakout season.

Suddenly, that all seemed to fall apart. In the Rams' third preseason game, Green suffered a season-ending knee injury. Now Vermeil had to turn to little-known backup Kurt Warner to run the Rams' high-powered offense.

Until then, Warner had been largely ignored in NFL circles. He had been undrafted out of the University of Northern Iowa. Warner's only

ISAAC BRUCE RACES AWAY FROM TITANS DEFENDERS TO COMPLETE A 73-YARD TOUCHDOWN PASS IN SUPER BOWL XXXIV.

professional football experience was in the Arena Football League and in the minor league NFL Europe. He even had to stock shelves for $5.50 an hour at a Hy-Vee grocery store in his native Cedar Falls, Iowa, to

CALMER COACH

Dick Vermeil was a less intense coach than he had been by the time he led the Rams to victory in Super Bowl XXXIV. But nearly two decades earlier, as the Philadelphia Eagles' coach, Vermeil was so dedicated to his job he would sleep in his office.

make ends meet. He had spent the 1998 season as the Rams' third-string quarterback.

Warner was an immediate success as a starter. He threw three touchdown passes in each of his first three starts—an NFL first. Then in his fourth game, against the San Francisco 49ers, Warner threw a touchdown pass in each of the Rams' first three possessions. He finished the game with five touchdown passes.

For the season, Warner had some of the best quarterback statistics ever. He completed 65.1 percent of his passes for 4,353 yards and 41 touchdowns. He won the NFL's Most Valuable Player (MVP) award. The Rams finished 13–3 and scored an amazing 526 points (32.9 per game) while allowing just 242.

Warner, Faulk, Bruce, Holt, and the rest of the Rams' offense became known as the "Greatest Show on Turf." The artificial turf at their home stadium, the Edward Jones Dome, allowed the players to move faster than on natural grass. The Rams especially took advantage of the speedy turf in the playoffs.

In their first game of the playoffs, the Rams overpowered

HE SAID IT

"How can you be in awe of something that you expect yourself to do? People think this season is the first time I touched a football; they don't realize I've been doing this for years—just not on this level, because I never got the chance. Sure, I had my tough times, but you don't sit there and say, 'Wow, I was stocking groceries five years ago, and look at me now.' You don't think about it, and when you do achieve something, you know luck has nothing to do with it."

— *Kurt Warner after Super Bowl XXXIV*

RAMS QUARTERBACK KURT WARNER ROLLS OUT OF THE POCKET IN SEARCH OF A RECEIVER IN SUPER BOWL XXXIV.

the Minnesota Vikings by a score of 49–37. Next, in the National Football Conference (NFC) Championship Game, the Rams won a tight game 11–6 over the Tampa Bay Buccaneers. The team that had struggled for so many years was on its way to Super Bowl XXXIV.

The Rams' dramatic season continued until the very end of the Super Bowl against the Tennessee Titans. At the Georgia Dome in Atlanta, Georgia, the Rams took a 16–0 third quarter lead. But the Titans came back in the fourth quarter. Tennessee

SEE YA, KURT

Kurt Warner finally retired after the 2009 season. He was 38 years old. After being released by the Rams in 2003, Warner joined the New York Giants and then the Arizona Cardinals. After the 2008 season, Warner led the Cardinals to their first Super Bowl. He finished his career with 32,344 yards passing (.655 percentage), 208 touchdown passes, and 128 interceptions.

running back Eddie George scored two touchdowns. A two-point conversion after the first touchdown had failed. But the Titans added a field goal to tie the game with only 2:12 left.

With momentum now firmly on the Titans' side, Warner led the Rams offense onto the field. On the first play of the drive, Warner hit Bruce for a 73-yard touchdown strike. The Rams took a 23–16 lead.

The Titans did not quit. They took over with 1:48 left and drove down the field. With six seconds left, Tennessee had the ball on the Rams' 10-yard line. The final play of Super Bowl XXXIV was one of the most dramatic plays in Super Bowl history.

The Titans would need to score on this final play in order to tie the game. Tennessee

RAMS LINEBACKER MIKE JONES WRAPS UP TITANS RECEIVER KEVIN DYSON, KEEPING HIM OUT OF THE END ZONE AT THE END OF SUPER BOWL XXXIV.

quarterback Steve McNair took the snap and dropped back to find a receiver. He quickly found wide receiver Kevin Dyson just off to the right. Dyson caught the ball on the run near the 5-yard line. As he turned and tried to force his way into the end zone, Rams linebacker Mike Jones wrapped him up. Dyson stretched, but he could not quite reach the end zone. The "Greatest Show on Turf" finally brought a Super Bowl to the Rams franchise and to St. Louis.

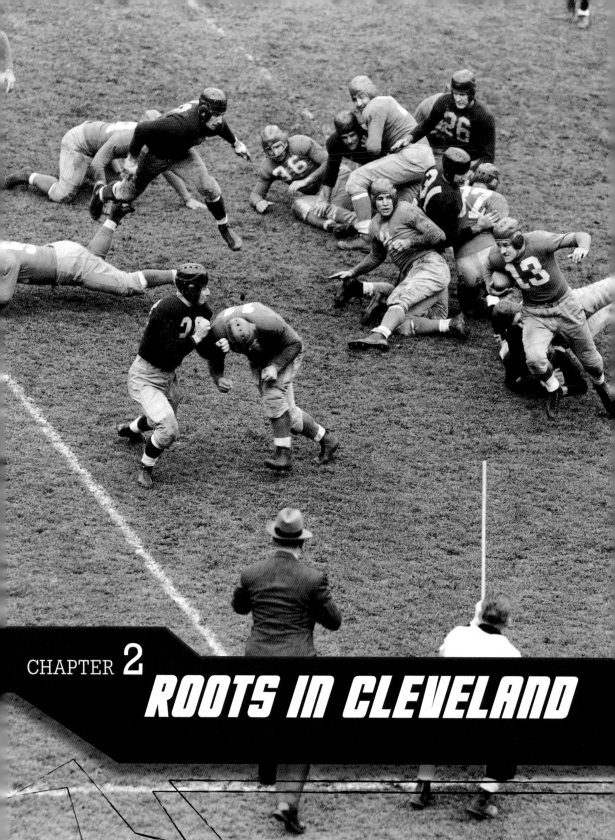

CHAPTER 2

ROOTS IN CLEVELAND

The Great Depression crippled many businesses during the 1930s. When the U.S. economy was at its all-time worst, some teams in the new NFL were just beginning. The Pittsburgh Steelers began playing in 1933. Four years later, another industrial town hard-hit by the downturn welcomed an NFL team. The team was called the Cleveland Rams.

On February 13, 1937, the NFL granted a team to Homer Marshman and Associates for $10,000. The group of Cleveland, Ohio, businessmen became the first owners of the Rams. Marshman, an attorney, adopted the Rams nickname because his general manager, Buzz Wetzel, liked the Fordham University Rams. Marshman liked how the name "Rams" sounded.

M-V-P!

Rams quarterback Parker Hall led the NFL in pass completions in 1939, earning the league's Most Valuable Player award.

THE RAMS PLAYERS, IN DARK JERSEYS, DEFEND AGAINST THE NEW YORK GIANTS IN A 1938 GAME AT THE POLO GROUNDS IN NEW YORK.

Hugo Bezdek was hired as the Rams' first coach. The team's first game was against the Detroit Lions at Cleveland's Municipal Stadium on September 10, 1937. The Lions won 28–0. The first Rams team finished just 1–10 in its first season. The Rams alternated between League Park and Shaw Stadium, a high school field, in 1938. They moved back to Municipal Stadium the next year.

In 1939, Dutch Clark took over as the Rams' coach. Clark had been a big-name coach for the Lions. In his first year, the Rams improved to 5–5–1. But that was the team's best record during this period. The Rams were sold in 1941 to partners Dan Reeves and Fred Levy. Then, play was interrupted by World War II. Reeves and Levy joined the U.S. Army Air Corps, though they retained ownership of the team.

Due to the huge number of players away in military service, the Rams suspended operations for the 1943 season. They resumed in 1944, but their war-depleted roster produced another losing record. The Rams were 25–49–1 overall in their short existence up to 1944.

Things started to look up beginning with the 1944 draft. In the fifth round, the Rams picked University of California, Los Angeles (UCLA), star

THE CLEVELAND BROWNS

Many people believed that famed coach Paul Brown would take over the Rams after the 1945 season. Rams owner Dan Reeves denied those rumors. Instead, Brown began a team named after himself in the new All-America Conference. Eventually the Cleveland Browns joined the NFL. The original Cleveland Browns moved to Baltimore, Maryland, and became the Ravens before the 1996 season. However, before the 1999 season, the NFL awarded a new team to Cleveland. The new team took on the Browns' name, colors, and history.

FROM LEFT, THE RAMS' CORBY DAVIS, RUDY MUCHA, JOHNNY DRAKE, AND PARKER HALL POSE FOR A PICTURE IN 1941.

quarterback Bob Waterfield. He returned from military service and joined the Rams for the 1945 season. Waterfield quickly meshed with his new teammates.

Coach Adam Walsh guided his more talented team to a 4–0 start in 1945. The Rams dominated the powerful Chicago Bears for two of those victories. Then, on November 22, the Rams clinched their first Western Division title with a 28–21 win over the Lions in Detroit. Waterfield threw 10 passes for a then-record 303 yards to his favorite target, receiver Jim Benton. And he did it all in pain.

"Bob suffered muscle injuries in his side," owner Reeves said later. "Until the day of the Detroit game he couldn't raise

EARNING HIS PAY

Bob Waterfield's championship-season play in 1945 earned him the richest contract in the NFL at the time. Owner Dan Reeves gave him $60,000 for three years, beginning with the 1946 season.

Waterfield earned his pay. Nicknamed "The Rifle" for his strong arm, he also doubled as a defensive back his first four seasons. He even intercepted 20 passes. During the middle part of the century, quarterbacks often handled place-kicking and punting duties. Waterfield kicked 60 field goals during his career and more than 300 extra points.

"Waterfield is the best, the trickiest and the most valuable operator in the league," wrote *New York Times* columnist Arthur Daley. "Waterfield is not only a consummate magician as a quarterback, but he is a solid punter."

Waterfield retired after the 1952 season and was inducted into the Pro Football Hall of Fame in 1965.

his right arm. We gave him a couple of shots to deaden the pain. You know what he did to the Lions."

Waterfield threw 14 touchdown passes in 10 regular season games that season. He was helped by a strong backfield that included running backs Fred Gehrke, Jim Gillette, Don Greenwood, and Albie Reisz. His main receiver, Benton, racked up 1,067 yards.

The Rams finished the regular season 9–1. In the NFL Championship Game, they faced the Washington Redskins on December 16 in a snow-filled Municipal Stadium. The day was so cold—just 2 degrees—that players covered themselves in hay while on the sidelines to keep warm.

A crowd of 32,178 fans showed up for the game. The

RAMS RUNNING BACK DON GREENWOOD (66), HANGS ONTO THE BALL AS HE IS TACKLED BY A WASHINGTON REDSKINS PLAYER IN 1945.

Rams fans who braved the chill got to see Waterfield throw a 37-yard pass to Benton for a touchdown. They also saw him throw a 44-yard pass to Gillette for another score. The Rams then held on for a tight 15–14 victory and an NFL title.

The Rams soon would win another NFL title, but it was 2,500 miles (4,023 km) away from Cleveland. The team would soon begin a journey crisscrossing the country to find its new home base.

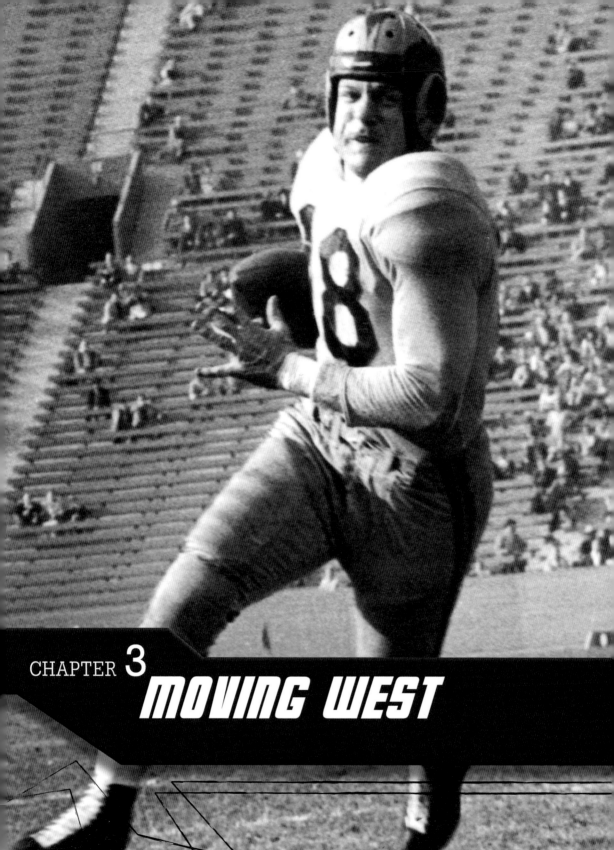

CHAPTER 3 MOVING WEST

Controversy brewed while the Rams celebrated their 1945 NFL championship. Owner Dan Reeves denied reports that he would move his training camp to Los Angeles, California, or any other locations that were far from Cleveland. Little did the public know that Reeves had already made plans to move the team to Los Angeles.

The team had endured disappointing attendance in Cleveland. Reeves hoped Los Angeles would be better. The city in Southern California had seen a major economic and population boom during World War II.

Reeves announced the West Coast move just one month after the title win over the Washington Redskins. The Rams would become the first major-league sports team to play in Los

DID YOU KNOW?

The Rams were the first NFL team to employ a full-time scouting staff and the first to issue face masks for their players.

LOS ANGELES RAMS RUNNING BACK FRED GEHRKE WAS RESPONSIBLE FOR PAINTING THE TRADEMARK HORNS ON THE RAMS HELMET.

FIVE MEMBERS OF THE 1946 LOS ANGELES RAMS WERE FROM UCLA, INCLUDING KENNY WASHINGTON (13) AND WOODY STROBE (34).

Angeles. There, they would play home games in the 100,000-seat Los Angeles Coliseum. The massive stadium had been built for the 1932 Olympic Games.

Although the stadium offered seemingly unlimited seating capacity, the team faced challenges on the West Coast.

In 1946, the nearest NFL team to the Rams was more than 2,000 miles (3,219 km) away. Travel was time-consuming. Cross-country trains took two or three days. Propeller-driven airplanes—half as fast as modern jets—used up most of one day and usually required a stop or two to get to the East Coast. To solve the problem, Reeves offered $5,000 to opponents who would play the Rams in Los Angeles.

The Los Angeles Rams became innovators in other ways, as well. Beginning in 1934, the NFL had only allowed white players into the league. But in 1946, Reeves signed African-American running backs Kenny Washington and Woody Strode. They were the first black players to play in the NFL since the ban 12 years earlier. One year later, Jackie Robinson would break the color barrier in Major League Baseball, becoming the first black major leaguer.

Reeves did not stop with Washington and Strode. The Rams became pro sports' most integrated team. They soon added running backs "Deacon Dan" Towler and Tank Younger, along with defensive stars

Dick "Night Train" Lane and Bob Boyd. Towler and Younger teamed with Dick Hoerner to form the "Bull Elephant" backfield. Each player weighed at least 225 pounds—which in those days was about the size of an average lineman.

Meanwhile, the team added star receivers Elroy "Crazylegs" Hirsch and Tom Fears for Bob Waterfield to throw to. Coach Clark Shaughnessy guided the team to the Western Division title in 1949. However, the Rams lost 14–0 to the Philadelphia Eagles in the NFL Championship Game. Former Bears star lineman Joe Stydahar replaced Shaughnessy as coach in 1950. But the Rams were frustrated again in the NFL Championship Game. They lost 30–28 to the Cleveland Browns.

The Rams were football's top offensive team in 1950.

CRAZYLEGS

Elroy "Crazylegs" Hirsch got his nickname for his zigzag running style while playing high school football. But he believed the name came from Chicago, Illinois, sportswriter Francis Powers. "Whatever, I certainly didn't mind it. In fact, I think it helped," Hirsch said.

The Rams drafted Hirsch in 1945, but he played his first three seasons with the Chicago Rockets of the All-America Football Conference. He was a running back when he first came to the Rams. Then he became a full-time wide receiver just in time for the title run in 1951. "Crazylegs" became known for catching long passes on the run with his fingertips. They were called the "Elroy Hirsch Special."

Hirsch stayed on with the Rams after his retirement in 1957. He was general manager from 1960 to 1969. Hirsch then went back to his home state to be athletic director at the University of Wisconsin.

They even scored 70 points in one game. In 1949, they had drafted quarterback Norm Van Brocklin. He split time with Waterfield in 1951 but still put up big numbers. In the season opener, Van Brocklin threw for a record 554 yards against the now-defunct New York Yanks. "We were so explosive that a game never was really over as long as we had a couple of chances left," said Younger.

Waterfield was still an effective player, helping the Rams pull off some major comebacks that season. But he also needed Van Brocklin's help. Complementing each other, the quarterbacks helped lead the Rams to an 8–4 regular season. Waterfield and Van Brocklin each threw 13 touchdown

ELROY "CRAZYLEGS" HIRSCH WAS KNOWN FOR HIS ABILITY TO CATCH LONG BOMBS.

passes. Hirsch gained 1,495 receiving yards while Fears caught 18 passes in one game.

"We both had our pride, and we both naturally liked playing as much as possible," said Waterfield. "But under the circumstances, I think it worked out very well."

On December 23, 1951, the Rams met the Cleveland Browns again in the NFL Championship Game. Although the Rams' Waterfield/Van Brocklin-led offense was considered the league's best, the Browns were not far behind. Their quarterback, Otto Graham, guided a high-powered offense that included receivers Dub Jones, Mac Speedie, and Dante Lavelli as well as running back Marion Motley. Even their kicker, Lou Groza, was among the most accurate in the league.

More than 57,520 fans showed up at the Coliseum to see the NFL Championship Game rematch. The three star quarterbacks were largely held in check throughout the game. But the break came midway through the fourth quarter. After replacing Waterfield in the third quarter, Van Brocklin hit Fears for a 73-yard touchdown pass in the fourth. That broke a 17–17 tie. As the clock ticked to zero, hundreds of Rams fans ran onto the field to celebrate with their heroes. With a 24–17 win, the Rams had won their first NFL Championship since moving to Los Angeles.

Even with Van Brocklin's long touchdown pass, the coach praised the Rams' defense. "We kept the pressure on Otto Graham all the time," Stydahar said. "We gave him a bad time, rushing in our linebackers as

QUARTERBACK BOB WATERFIELD GUIDED THE RAMS' FEARED OFFENSE FROM 1945–52. HE THREW FOR 97 CAREER TOUCHDOWNS.

well as our line when he threw. In that last quarter, especially, we had the Browns upset the way we mixed up our defenses."

The early Los Angeles Rams teams had loads of talent and an NFL title within their first five years. But despite their talent and early success, the 1951 title would be the last in the team's history in Southern California.

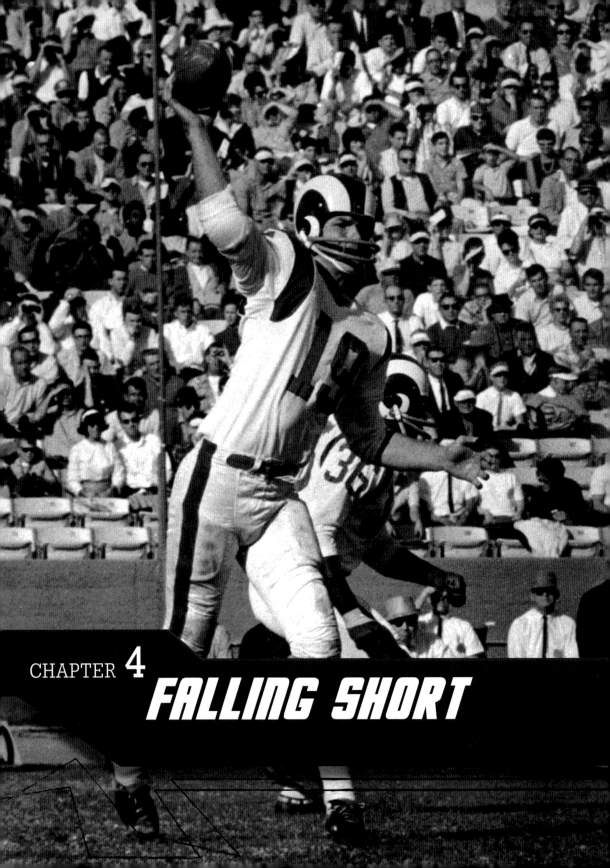

CHAPTER 4

FALLING SHORT

The Rams continued to be high-scoring title contenders for the first half of the 1950s. Under coach Sid Gillman, the Rams even made the 1955 NFL Championship Game. But they lost 38–14 to the Cleveland Browns. After that, the Rams began a long decline. They recorded only one winning season (8–4 in 1958) through 1965.

Although the Rams were not successful on the field, they remained popular in Los Angeles. The team drew an NFL record crowd of 102,368 for a victory over the San Francisco 49ers in 1957. They averaged 74,296 fans per game that year.

In 1959, the Rams traded nine players to the Chicago Cardinals for star running back Ollie Matson. The deal was completed by Rams general manager Pete Rozelle. He would later become NFL commissioner. In 1960, Bob Waterfield took over as

RAMS QUARTERBACK BILL MUNSON FIRES A PASS DURING A 1964 GAME AGAINST THE MINNESOTA VIKINGS.

Rams coach. But Waterfield and Matson could not guide the Rams to a winning season.

In the NFL, the teams with the worst records get the highest draft picks. That was the case for the Rams in the early 1960s. In 1962, they picked defensive tackle Merlin Olsen and quarterback Roman Gabriel in the first round. They joined linemen David "Deacon" Jones and Lamar Lundy. Jones and Lundy had been acquired in 1961 and 1957 respectively. Star tackle Roosevelt Grier came over from the New York Giants in 1963.

ROMAN GABRIEL

Roman Gabriel threw 25 touchdown passes in 1967 and 24 in 1969. Gabriel helped make the Rams one of the strongest teams in the NFL with 11 wins in both seasons. But he did not have his greatest overall season until he was traded to the Philadelphia Eagles in 1973. That year, Gabriel threw for a personal-best 3,219 yards.

The building blocks for a successful team were in place. In 1966, Rams owner Dan Reeves hired George Allen to take over as Rams coach. Allen had been the defensive coordinator and draft guru of the Chicago Bears. The Olsen-Jones-Lundy-Grier defensive line soon became known as the "Fearsome Foursome." They fronted a strong, all-veteran defense. Allen had little tolerance for rookies, who took more time to develop.

"I like men with bald heads," Allen said. "I want to win today. I don't want to wait for tomorrow."

Allen surrounded Gabriel with veteran offensive linemen. He also had wide receiver Jack Snow and running back Willie Ellison to work with. The 1966 Rams finished 8–6. Many fans expected the team to take a big step forward the next season.

FROM LEFT, THE "FEARSOME FOURSOME" OF MERLIN OLSEN, LAMAR LUNDY, DEACON JONES, AND ROGER BROWN CLOSE IN ON THE COLTS IN 1967.

And they did. The 1967 Rams became a dominant team, finishing 11–1–2. However, they drew a tough matchup in the playoffs. They would face the Green Bay Packers, who were nearing the end of their famed dynasty of great teams. On Green Bay's frozen turf, the Packers won 28–7.

The Rams won 30 games from 1968 to 1970 under Allen. But they made the playoffs just once. They lost to the

FEARSOME LONGEVITY

There was only one change in the "Fearsome Foursome" of the 1960s. Roger Brown replaced Rosey Grier, who was forced into retirement by a ruptured Achilles tendon.

RAMS QUARTERBACK JAMES HARRIS (12) AND RUNNING BACK LAWRENCE MCCUTCHEON (30) AFTER A MCCUTCHEON TOUCHDOWN IN 1975

Minnesota Vikings in 1969. Allen was fired, and the team declined further under new coach Tommy Prothro. A strange off-the-field trade took place in 1972 on July 14. Longtime owner Dan Reeves had died at 58 in 1971. His successor was Robert Irsay. He was a Chicago heating and air-conditioning executive. Irsay swapped the entire Rams franchise for that of the Baltimore Colts. The Colts were owned by Carroll Rosenbloom. The players of each team stayed put, but the owners flip-flopped.

As one of many changes, Rosenbloom hired Chuck Knox as coach for the 1973 season. He also added veteran

John Hadl at quarterback and Lawrence McCutcheon, a perennial 1,000-yard rusher, at running back. The Rams were again dominant in the regular season, finishing 12–2. But they were knocked out in the playoffs again, this time 26–17 by Roger Staubach and the Dallas Cowboys.

The Rams had integrated the NFL back in 1946. In 1974, the Rams again set the pace for minority advancement in the game. The team started the season 3–2 behind Hadl's inconsistent play. So Knox started backup James Harris against the San Francisco 49ers on October 20, 1974, at the Los Angeles Coliseum. Harris became the first black quarterback to regularly start in the NFL. He went on to craft a 37–14 victory that day. He was 12-for-15 passing for 276 yards

GEORGE ALLEN

George Allen had a strange, three-part coaching career with the Rams. He was first offered the job in 1966. It was common for teams to allow an assistant to break a contract for a head coaching job. However, the Chicago Bears would not let him break his contract as an assistant coach. The Bears sued Allen before finally releasing him.

After three seasons with the Rams, Allen had conflicts with team owner Dan Reeves and was fired. But fans picketed the Rams' office and 7,500 signed a petition to bring him back. He was rehired in January but was fired again after two seasons. Allen was hired again in 1977. New owner Carroll Rosenbloom soon regretted that decision. Allen preferred veteran players, so he began getting rid of the team's young, talented players. He was fired for the third time after two preseason games in 1978.

and three touchdowns. Harris also quarterbacked the Rams' first playoff victory since 1951. They beat the Washington Redskins 19–10. But the Rams fell short in their bid to reach their first Super Bowl. They lost to the Minnesota Vikings 14–10 in the NFC Championship Game.

Knox and the Rams continued to be frustrated from 1975 to 1977. They won the Western Division each year, but always fell short in the playoffs. Ray Malavasi took over as coach in 1978 and suffered the same result. But 1979 would turn out to be perhaps the strangest year in Rams history. It also produced their first trip to the Super Bowl—and an ultimate near miss.

Negative news hurt the Rams even before the 1979 season began. On April 2, Rosenbloom died in a mysterious drowning accident. Regular quarterback Pat Haden broke his hand on a teammate's helmet. Replacement Bob Lee, acquired from the Minnesota Vikings, was injured in his second game. The Rams were forced to turn to third-stringer Vince Ferragamo. The Rams won five of their final seven games to finish 9–7 and sneak into the playoffs. There, they upset the Dallas Cowboys 21–19. Then Los Angeles edged out the Tampa Bay Buccaneers 9–0 in the NFC Championship Game. They would face the three-time champion Pittsburgh Steelers at Super Bowl XIV.

"Not even a Hollywood astrologer could have predicted this," said Malavasi.

The Rams got to play the big game at home in front of many of their own fans. More than 103,000 crammed into the Rose Bowl in nearby Pasadena,

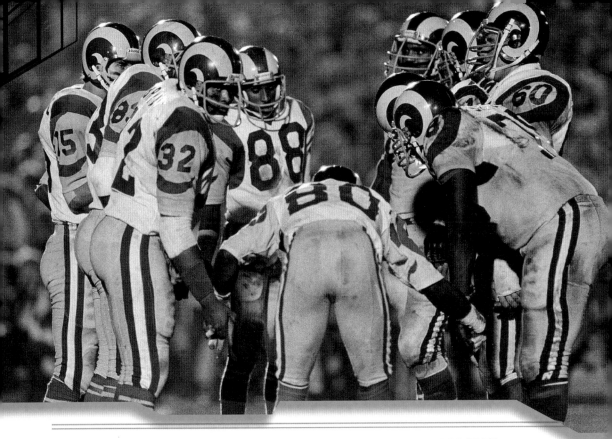

THE RAMS OFFENSE HUDDLES DURING SUPER BOWL XIV. THEY LOST TO THE PITTSBURGH STEELERS 31–19.

California, on January 20, 1980. The Rams led 13–10 at halftime. McCutcheon threw a 24-yard touchdown pass to Ron Smith on a trick play. That gave the Rams a 19–17 lead going into the fourth quarter. But Pittsburgh's star quarterback Terry Bradshaw tossed a 73-yard touchdown pass to John Stallworth to give the Steelers the lead. Running back Franco Harris scored an insurance touchdown, and the Steelers won 31–19.

"There was no loser today," Bradshaw said. "Both teams deserved the title. The Rams are one tough club."

Unfortunately, consolations like that kept coming the Rams' way for another two decades.

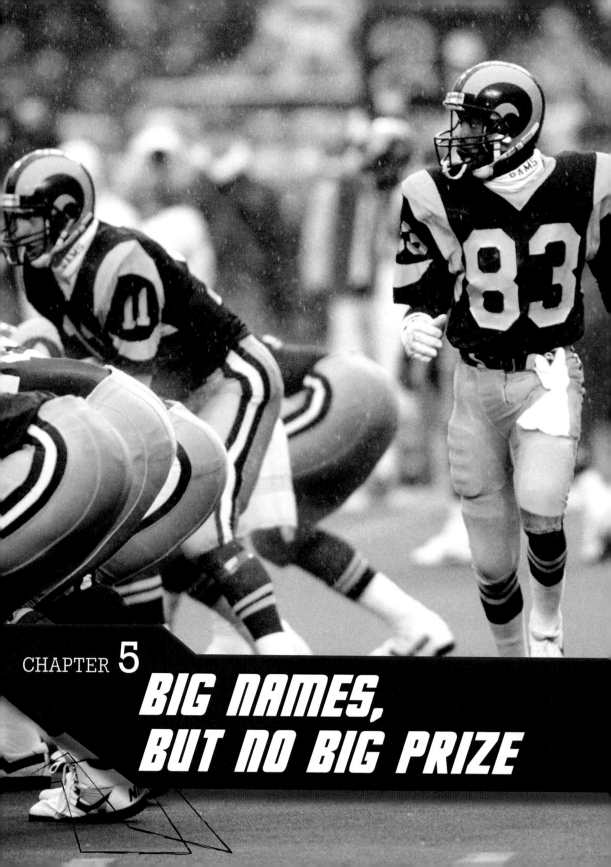

CHAPTER 5

BIG NAMES, BUT NO BIG PRIZE

The Rams' Cinderella season in 1979 had just a short carryover. The team moved down the freeway to Anaheim Stadium for the 1980 season. They finished 11–5 but once again made a quick exit from the playoffs. The Rams went downhill after that. Coach Ray Malavasi was fired after the 1982 season.

When the Rams needed a new coach for the 1983 season, they went to the biggest name Southern California had to offer. They hired John Robinson. He had led the University of Southern California to three Pacific-10 Conference championships and one national championship.

Robinson quickly turned the team around. He built the team first around star running back Eric Dickerson. He then focused on quarterback Jim Everett in 1986. Between 1984 and 1989, the Rams won either 10 or 11 games in five of the six seasons.

QUARTERBACK JIM EVERETT (11) CALLS SIGNALS WHILE WIDE RECEIVER WILLIE ANDERSON (83) GOES IN MOTION DURING A 1989 PLAYOFF GAME.

The fans traveling to Anaheim Stadium had plenty of drama during the regular seasons. Dickerson had become the NFL's top running back immediately after he was drafted in the first round in 1983. He gained a league-leading 1,808 yards in his rookie season. Then he really stepped on the gas in the 1984 season. Dickerson rushed for an all-time record 2,105 yards. He averaged 131.6 yards per game and 5.6 yards per carry that season. Dickerson broke O. J. Simpson's all-time mark of 2,003 yards set in 1973.

A RUNNER FIRST

Eric Dickerson was one of the top running backs of all time. Unlike many running backs of his era, however, Dickerson did not catch many passes. Dickerson caught 51 passes his rookie year in 1983. But then he never snared more than 26 in any of his other three full seasons as a Ram. Dickerson was inducted into Pro Football's Hall of Fame in 1999.

"Running is so natural to me," Dickerson said. "When I was running track in high school, people used to ask me, 'When are you going to start running hard?' The wind hits me in the face, and I feel so smoooooth. Man I love to run."

"It's shocking how good he is," Robinson exclaimed. "Really shocking."

But the Rams lacked a top quarterback to complement Dickerson, who had another 1,800-yard season in 1986. The quarterback position became a revolving door until the Rams traded for the 6-foot-5 Jim Everett in 1986. There was one problem with his arrival: Dickerson did not stick around long enough for Everett to mature. Just as soon as Everett became the starter in 1987, Dickerson became dissatisfied with his contract. He demanded a trade and

RAMS RUNNING BACK ERIC DICKERSON FINDS SPACE TO RUN DURING A
1986 WIN OVER THE ATLANTA FALCONS.

was dealt to the Indianapolis Colts in midseason 1987.

Everett became the Rams' star. He led the NFL with 31 touchdown passes in 1988. Receiver Henry Ellard was a favorite target. Running back Greg Bell, whom the Rams got in the Dickerson trade, became a big contributor. He had 1,212 rush-ing yards and an NFL-leading 16 touchdowns. The Rams had one more good regular season but then began to decline.

During all of those successful seasons, the Rams only made it to the NFC Championship Game twice. They lost to the Chicago Bears 24–0 in January 1986. Then they lost to their archrival, the San Francisco 49ers, 30–3 in January 1989. Once again, a Super Bowl championship was frustratingly elusive.

As the Rams declined, attendance in Anaheim dropped, too. Owner Georgia Frontiere was unable to get a new stadium built anywhere in the area. So she looked to her hometown of St. Louis, Missouri, for a possible new home for the Rams.

The deal was made. The Edward Jones Dome (originally known as the Trans World Dome) was under construction in downtown St. Louis. It would be available for the Rams and would have all the updated features desired in a modern stadium. After 49 years in the Los Angeles area, the Rams moved to St. Louis in 1995.

While construction finished on the Trans World Dome, the Rams temporarily played in Busch Stadium. That is where the St. Louis Cardinals baseball team played. The Trans World Dome opened on November 12, 1995. The Rams defeated the Carolina Panthers 28–17 in their first game. It was a high point in a 7–9 season. Wide receiver Isaac Bruce was only a second-year player in 1995. In a sign of what was to come, he starred with 119 receptions that year.

After a bumpy season, much better days were just a few years away. The arrival of Kurt

TOP QB?

Jim Everett once said, "I just want to be remembered as the best quarterback the Rams have had . . . and that won't come easy." His stature in Los Angeles may be up for debate, but statistically he is the best in Rams history. He is the passing-yardage leader with 23,758. That is about 1,000 more yards than Roman Gabriel. Kurt Warner had 14,447 yards with the Rams. Everett completed 56.4 percent of his passes and threw 142 touchdowns.

WIDE RECEIVER TORRY HOLT OF THE ST. LOUIS RAMS CELEBRATES AFTER SCORING A TOUCHDOWN IN 1999.

Warner and the emergence of the "Greatest Show on Turf" made the Rams one of the most feared teams in the NFL. Their success did not stop after the victory in Super Bowl XXXIV.

Coach Dick Vermiel retired after the 1999 season and was replaced by Mike Martz. Under Martz, the team's prolific offense upped their 1999 total by scoring 540 points in 2000. However, injuries slowed the team down. They finished 10–6 and lost in the first round of the playoffs.

But they were back in 2001. Warner led the Rams to a team-best 14–2 regular-season record.

He was also named the league's MVP while Faulk was the Offensive Player of the Year. After winning two playoff games, the Rams met the New England Patriots in Super Bowl XXXVI. Like the Rams' previous Super Bowl appearance, this one came down to the final play. But this time it did not go the Rams' way. Patriots kicker Adam Vinatieri made a field goal as time expired. The Patriots won 20–17 in what was considered a big upset.

The Rams' roster began to change after the 2001 season. The team started the 2002 season 0–5. Warner had played poorly and then became injured during that time. In his place, Marc Bulger emerged and eventually took over the full-time starting job. Bulger led the Rams to a 12–4 record in 2003. He was later selected to two Pro Bowls. In 2004, the Rams drafted run-

ORLANDO PACE

In 1997, the Rams drafted Ohio State University offensive tackle Orlando Pace with the first overall pick. Pace went on to become one of the top offensive linemen in the game. He also played a big part in helping the Rams reach two Super Bowls. Pace was selected to seven straight Pro Bowls beginning in 1999. He stayed with the Rams until 2009, when he was released for salary cap reasons.

ning back Steven Jackson. He rushed for more than 1,000 yards in five straight seasons from 2005 to 2009. Wide receiver Torry Holt remained the team's leading receiver from his second year with the team in 2000 until his last year in 2008.

Despite some talented offensive players, the Rams were never able to recapture the team-wide dominance they had from 1999 until 2001. As the stars from their heyday began retiring or moving to other teams, the Rams struggled to replace them through the draft and free

RAMS RUNNING BACK STEVEN JACKSON, SHOWN IN 2009, RUSHED FOR MORE THAN 1,000 YARDS EVERY SEASON FROM 2005 TO 2009.

agency. From 2002 to 2009, the Rams had only one winning season. In 2009, they finished a league-worst 1–15 and barely resembled the team that had dominated just 10 years before.

Through the Rams struggles, the team has been able to add talented young players through high draft picks. In 2010, the team selected quarterback Sam Bradford with the first overall pick in the NFL Draft.

With that, Rams fans hoped that Bradford and the other young players would develop into the next Warner, Faulk, Holt, and Bruce, so the team could once again be known as the "Greatest Show on Turf."

TIMELINE

1937	The Rams play their first game on September 10 in Cleveland, losing to the Detroit Lions 28–0.
1943	The Rams suspend operations for one season due to World War II.
1945	The Rams win their first NFL title at frozen Cleveland Stadium on December 16 in a 15–14 win over the Washington Redskins.
1946	Rams owner Dan Reeves announces on January 11 that the team is moving to Los Angeles.
1946	Playing their first game in Los Angeles on September 29, the Rams beat the Philadelphia Eagles 25–14.
1951	The Rams beat the Browns 24–17 on December 23 for their first and only NFL championship in Los Angeles.
1957	An NFL-record 102,368 watch the Rams outscore the San Francisco 49ers 37–24 on November 10 at the Los Angeles Coliseum.
1967	The great turnaround 11–1–2 season under George Allen ends in a 28–7 playoff loss on December 23 to the Super Bowl-bound Green Bay Packers.
1974	The Rams' James Harris becomes the first black quarterback to win an NFL playoff game on December 22.
1979	Rams owner Carroll Rosenbloom dies in a drowning accident on April 2. Wife Georgia Frontiere takes over as owner.

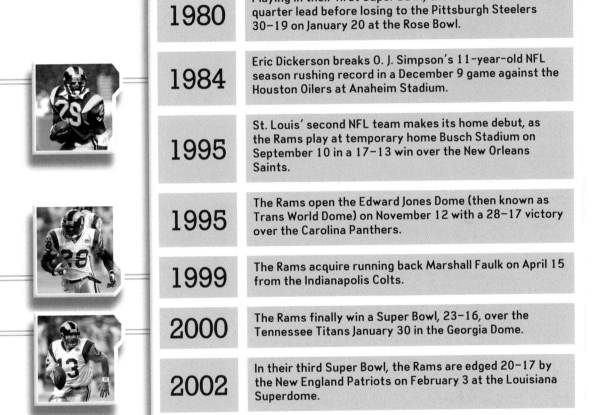

1980	Playing in their first Super Bowl, the Rams have a fourth-quarter lead before losing to the Pittsburgh Steelers 30–19 on January 20 at the Rose Bowl.
1984	Eric Dickerson breaks O. J. Simpson's 11-year-old NFL season rushing record in a December 9 game against the Houston Oilers at Anaheim Stadium.
1995	St. Louis' second NFL team makes its home debut, as the Rams play at temporary home Busch Stadium on September 10 in a 17–13 win over the New Orleans Saints.
1995	The Rams open the Edward Jones Dome (then known as Trans World Dome) on November 12 with a 28–17 victory over the Carolina Panthers.
1999	The Rams acquire running back Marshall Faulk on April 15 from the Indianapolis Colts.
2000	The Rams finally win a Super Bowl, 23–16, over the Tennessee Titans January 30 in the Georgia Dome.
2002	In their third Super Bowl, the Rams are edged 20–17 by the New England Patriots on February 3 at the Louisiana Superdome.
2003	Under head coach Mike Martz, the Rams have their last winning season for the decade, going 12–4.
2010	The Rams select quarterback Sam Bradford with the first overall pick in the NFL Draft.

QUICK STATS

FRANCHISE HISTORY
Cleveland Rams 1937–45
Los Angeles Rams 1946–94
St. Louis Rams 1995–

SUPER BOWLS
(wins in bold)
1979 (XIV), **1999 (XXXIV)**,
   2001 (XXXVI)

NFL CHAMPIONSHIP GAMES
(1937–69; wins in bold)
1945, 1949, 1950, **1951**, 1955

NFC CHAMPIONSHIP GAMES
(since 1970 AFL-NFL merger)
1974, 1975, 1976, 1978, 1979, 1985,
   1989, 1999, 2001

DIVISION CHAMPIONSHIPS
(since 1970 AFL-NFL merger)
1973, 1974, 1975, 1976, 1977, 1978,
   1979, 1985, 1999, 2001, 2003

KEY PLAYERS
(position, seasons with team)
Isaac Bruce (WR, 1994–2007)
Eric Dickerson (RB, 1983–87)
Jim Everett (QB, 1986–93)
Marshall Faulk (RB, 1999–2005)
Tom Fears (WR, 1948–56)
Elroy "Crazylegs" Hirsch
   (RB–WR, 1949–57)
Torry Holt (WR, 1999–2008)
Deacon Jones (DE, 1961–71)
Merlin Olsen (DT, 1962–76)
Norm Van Brocklin (QB, 1949–57)
Kurt Warner (QB, 1998–2003)
Bob Waterfield (QB, 1945–52)
Jack Youngblood (DE, 1971–84)

KEY COACHES
George Allen (1966–70):
   49–17–4; 0–2 (playoffs)
Dick Vermeil (1997–99):
   22–26; 3–0 (playoffs)

HOME FIELDS
Edward Jones Dome (1995–)
Busch Stadium (1995)
Anaheim Stadium (1980–94)
Los Angeles Coliseum (1946–79)
Shaw Stadium (1938)
League Park (1937, 1942, 1944–45)
Municipal Stadium
   (1937, 1939–1941, 1945)

* All statistics through 2009 season

QUOTES AND ANECDOTES

The signature rams-horn design on the Rams' helmets originated with running back Fred Gehrke in 1947. An art major in college, Gehrke painted the yellow horn on a leather helmet. Eventually he painted 70 helmets. The Rams thus became the first pro team to feature a logo on their helmets. Today, only the Cleveland Browns lack a helmet logo in the NFL.

The Rams did not have to "go Hollywood" because they already were there. Many players ended up having movie and TV acting careers that lasted longer than their time in football. Among the Rams players who also starred in Hollywood were Bob Waterfield, Elroy "Crazylegs" Hirsch, Woody Strode, Bernie Casey, Roosevelt Grier, Merlin Olsen, Fred Dryer, and Roman Gabriel.

Hirsch played himself in a 1953 movie *Crazylegs*. He then played the airline pilot in the 1957 movie *Zero Hour* that became the model for pilot Peter Graves in the 1980 comedy *Airplane*. Olsen co-starred in the TV series *Little House on the Prairie*, then starred in his own series, *Father Murphy*. Strode, one of the first two postwar black players in the NFL, also was one of the earliest featured black actors starting in the mid-1950s. His most famous role was as John Wayne's sidekick in *The Man Who Shot Liberty Valance* in 1962.

Irv Cross, a Rams defensive back from 1966 to 1968, went on to star in the ensemble cast with Brent Musburger, Phyllis George, and Jimmy "The Greek" Snyder on CBS-TV's *The NFL Today* pregame and postgame shows in the 1980s.

Ron Brown impressed the world with a gold medal for the United States' 400-meter relay team at the 1984 Olympics at the Los Angeles Coliseum. Brown then took his speed to the NFL, and the Rams acquired him to team with the great Henry Ellard at wide receiver.

GLOSSARY

contender

A team that is considered good enough to win a championship.

contract

A binding agreement about, for example, years of commitment by a football player in exchange for a given salary.

draft

A system used by professional sports leagues to select new players in order to spread incoming talent among all teams.

franchise

An entire sports organization, including the players, coaches, and staff.

free agent

A player free to sign with any team of his choosing after his contract expires.

general manager

The top executive of a team in charge of acquiring players.

hall of fame

A place built to honor noteworthy achievements by athletes in their respective sports.

integrated

To include people from more than one race.

momentum

A continued strong performance based on recent success.

retire

To officially end one's career.

rookie

A first-year professional athlete.

salary cap

A specific amount of money a team can spend on player salaries, mandated by the NFL to prevent salaries from spiraling out of control.

wild card

Playoff berths given to the best remaining teams that did not win their respective divisions.

Further Reading

MacCambridge, Michael. *America's Game: The Epic Story of How Pro Football Captured a Nation*. New York: Random House, 2004.

Rains, Rob. *Marshall Faulk: Rushing to Glory*. Champaign, IL: Sports Publishing, 1999.

Sports Illustrated. *The Football Book Expanded Edition*. New York: Sports Illustrated Books, 2009.

Warner, Kurt, with Michael Silver. *All Things Possible*: *My Story of Faith, Football and the Miracle Season*. San Francisco, CA: Harper San Francisco, 2000.

Web Links

To learn more about the St. Louis Rams, visit ABDO Publishing Company online at **www.abdopublishing.com**. Web sites about the Rams are featured on our Book Links page. These links are routinely monitored and updated to provide the most current information available.

Places to Visit

Edward Jones Dome, St. Louis
901 N. Broadway
St. Louis, MO 63101
314-342-5201
www.stlouisrams.com/edwardjonesdome
The Dome is the Rams' home field. They play eight regular season games here each season.

Pro Football Hall of Fame
2121 George Halas Drive Northwest
Canton, OH 44708
330-456-8207
www.profootballhof.com
This hall of fame and museum highlights the greatest players and moments in the history of the National Football League. Twenty-three people affiliated with the Rams are enshrined, including Bob Waterfield, Elroy "Crazylegs" Hirsch, Norm Van Brocklin, and Eric Dickerson.

INDEX

About the Author

George Castle covered the 1985 Super Bowl champion Bears for NBC Sports and other media outlets. Castle has authored 11 sports books since 1998, hosts the syndicated weekly "Diamond Gems" radio show, and writes for a variety of print and online outlets.